Reviews

Patrick Dobbs writes in a tradition
stretches back to the eighteenth c
proclaims and reaffirms deep-rooted values and ways of
being that survived relatively unscathed until the mid
twentieth century, but that are now under serious threat
from modernisation and "innovative" farming methods. In a
resonant and distinctive poetic voice, Dobbs celebrates
farming practices that intertwine with the land he gains a
living from and commemorates a rural culture that coexisted
with that land and drew imaginative nourishment from it.
This volume reflects on a lifetime of experience that spans
the Atlantic Ocean, always to return to his Welsh upland
farm. By turns celebratory, compassionate, elegiac, and
trenchant, his poetry will appeal to anyone who cares for the
resonant legacy of Romantic poetry, who delights in the rich
lexicon of rural life, and who appreciates the importance of
conserving deep knowledge of specific environments and
ecologies. *Tales from a Mountain Farm* retrieves, revives, and
re-energises ways of being and doing that we would be
foolish to let go. Dobbs asks: "And will we leave some tales of
our own / When we too are forgotten?" The emphatic answer
is, "Yes, indeed he will!"

Helen May Williams

In this delicious combination of smoothly blended poetry and
prose, Patrick Dobbs encapsulates his hill farming experience.
Invoking nostalgia with many treasured memories of my own
formative years and inspiring his reader with a strange
harmony of contrasts betwixt exotic imagery and the rustic
reality of life still to be found today in Cefn Gwlad ar y Rhiw.
Fresh and invigorating he brings his characters to life, bursting
through the pages in words which express his love and
respect for the environment which enfolds his home in the
character building hills, the Carmarthenshire Fan, within
Mynydd Du.

While, perhaps, the farming experience must be lived to be fully understood, Patrick succeeds in giving the reader an insight into a unique way of life. One which is largely governed by the rugged nature and raw beauty of its surroundings, but also where exotic dreams almost creep into view. A sustaining nourishment to be savoured and enjoyed time and again.

Venerable W Roger Hughes

Patrick Dobbs is one of a rare breed; a farmer-poet who, like Wendell Berry and the late Dic Jones, writes with the authority of someone who has spent a lifetime working the land. *Tales from a Mountain Farm* is the story of a 'life well-lived', captured in vivid and descriptive poetry. Dobbs takes us on a fascinating journey, peopled with characters from the past; Sam Lee, Willie Bach, Dai John, forgotten names which Dobbs remembers with affection.

These are honest, direct pieces, rooted in the land, nature, and the hard graft of husbandry. Yet amongst poems of cows and geese, sheepdog trials and shearing-sheds are tender poems of regret; for lost love, missed opportunities, and the old ways of life.

This is a unique collection. Not just because it is one man's story, but because it's also a compelling account of farming in the Brecon Beacons, and customs which are rapidly disappearing. I read it with a sense of awe at Dobbs's tenacity, admiration for his carefully detailed poetry, and sadness at our vanishing traditions. In 'Llanddeusant Community Hall' Dobbs writes: 'Now is the time / To make some music of our own.' He has indeed made music.

Kathy Miles

Though these tales may be told *from* a mountain farm in Wales, they are tales *of* a world geography of adventure and a tribute to 80 years of farming. *Tales from a Mountain farm* is a recognition of the poet's place in a history of social change from the ancient to the future. Dobbs is a master storyteller and this collection reads like a series of programmes from the BBC world service.

Dobbs has chosen his own route all his life and reflecting on his journeys there is some sadness but no regret. There are outstanding poems of human relationships - *The Boundary 1986, Dai John, Wilson and me.* Poems that encapsulate the landscape of Wales from its Eastern to Western border or the continuity shared by the men who have nurtured and been nurtured by that landscape. There exists a constant tension in the poetry between traditional and modern, youth and age but the voice in which this is expressed is always tempered by experience, patience and tolerance.

The songs and stories celebrating the passage between the *Long walk to freedom* and *Cataracts* gathered carefully in this volume reach out from Wales to England, Canada, Scotland, Guyana and back again. There are tales of encounters with an Indian girl in Guyana, a beautiful blue-eyed blond from St Petersburg at a railway station in Zurich and with "Mandy of Roath" in the cafe outside B&Q.

To understand the reoccurring themes you may read *Hands on* almost as a summary of the entire book. *'my garden could tell you tales'* claims Dobbs toward the end of the collection, and reading this poem, you realise the poet and the poem, the farmer and the land are inseparable. I can sum up this collection in one of Dobbs most wonderful lines it is "a symphony of rhythm, sweat and muscle".

Dominic Williams

About the Author

Patrick Dobbs, sheep farmer, has been writing poems on and off all his life.   He earned his first fee of ten shillings and sixpence (nearly half his weekly wage in his first full-time farm job) for a poem published in the *Mickey Mouse* as a ten year old in 1945. He has found that the financial rewards for poetry has steadily declined from that day to this although his poems and stories have been broadcast and published in a variety of magazines and anthologies.

For nine years after leaving school he was an itinerant agricultural worker travelling through England, Ireland and Canada to Guyana, somehow acquiring a degree in agriculture from London University along the way.   Nearly sixty years ago he used his accumulated savings to buy a small mountain farm in the Brecon Beacons, and has survived there more or less happily ever since.

Patrick can be contacted via his page on Facebook
www.facebook.com/patrick.dobbs.39

Tales From A Mountain Farm

Patrick Dobbs

Cowry publishing

Published by Cowry Publishing
Gwisgo Ltd, 8 Sgwâr Alban, Aberaeron,
Ceredigion, SA46 0AD Wales, UK

www.cowrypublishing.co.uk

First published in September 2020

The right of Patrick Dobbs to be identified as the author
of this work has been asserted by him in accordance
with the Copyright, Designs and Patents Act of 1988.
Copyright Patrick Dobbs ©2020.
Printed and bound in Ceredigion by Gomer Press
Cover image: Stella Starnes
Cover design: Karen Gemma Brewer

A CIP catalogue record for this book is
available from the British Library

ISBN 978-1-908146-05-2

Dedication

**To the people
of Llanddeusant
who have put up with
my eccentricities
for nearly
sixty years.**

Acknowledgements

Some of these tales have appeared in a few magazines and anthologies, mostly of somewhat limited circulation.

I would like to thank all those who have given me such encouragement and said such kind words about my poems and stories over the years and the very generous comments that have been made about this particular collection.

I am particularly appreciative of Stella Starnes for her lovely picture on the front cover and more grateful than words can say for the work and enthusiasm put in by editor Karen Gemma Brewer who has kept production going forward in the daunting days of lockdown and distancing.

And I must thank Kathrin for sorting out my computer muddles as I tried to get these tales, some of which have been mouldering for decades on scraps of paper in dusty office drawers, into some kind of legible order.

Contents

Contents

Foreword by Karen Gemma Brewer

About time! A neat summary of reactions from poets on hearing this publication was in progress. It is a surprise that a Patrick Dobbs collection has not appeared before now, but I suppose it inevitably takes a lifetime to capture a generation of rural change. A rough chronology through the collection allows the reader to follow changes in the author as well as his landscape, rural life experienced through the arc of one rural life, walked gently on the back of a horse and teetered in a Land Rover over a precipice. Later poems employ increasing reflection, but there is little melancholy and much humour. Amongst rolling belly pork guffaws are gentle, soft-footed jibes and lulling tickles before the snatch of the trout. Romanticism is strongly evident too, naturally in a poetry of landscape, of place and of relationship. Patrick's poems reveal the buried endeavour of a drained field, sift out the quiet words of silent men and dally with his *'flowers of the field'* - beautiful women, cows, sheep and especially sheepdogs. Alongside disappearing skills, traditions and a whole way of living, Patrick's poems are bejewelled with nouns and verbs, such as *'hame'* and *'feather,'* so faded from the vernacular we have included a glossary.

Poet/Farmer/Traveller, a shared triumvirate between Patrick and I and although our first meeting is beyond recall, I well remember the first time we performed together, mind you, as very much separate acts. It was Carmarthen Old Town Festival, his rural radio voice rhythmically word perfect, rising to an angry crescendo drowned only by the roaring laughter of the audience. He whispered to me afterwards: "You were better than I expected!" and I realised his pre-performance worries were on the capability of his company! From there I believe grew the mutual respect that has brought these poems to my hands, an honour and responsibility this book aspires to meet. I dare to include here a poem I wrote on the eve of Patrick's 80th year, my attempt to portray his vivacity, slave to rhythm, sense of mischief and contrary contrasts.

At 79

Dear Patrick
it is a pat trick
to score four
yet carry three
like a tree
that hides its rings.

Here you tick
heartbeat iambic
scan your law
lines shackled free
like monkeys
learning to sing.

Elastic
rhymes in gymnastic
centaur sure
tap stepping glee
like donkeys
trampolining.

Over our years at Lampeter Writers' Workshop I have become
familiar with Patrick's work, his regular use of the word
'score' and many of the contrasts of his life and personality.
Solitary and social, stern and soft, quiet and proclaiming,
authoritative and enquiring, insistent and reserved, old-
fashioned and innovative, travelled and sessile. All the conflict
of a natural poet and that is only the minute portion I have
come to know of a man deep with experience from before my
conception. For all that is revealed in this collection, I am sure
there is more to come.

As years have passed, I have had the pleasure of performing
with Patrick on several stages, still as very much separate
acts. I first heard him perform the poem *'Without Regrets'* at
Llandeilo's Cawdor Hotel on a culture clashing rural Wales
meets urban Wales event featuring Lampeter Writers'

Workshop and Poets On The Hill - from Swansea. The poem affected all who attended that night, city and country dwellers alike. I have always loved it and I enjoyed the opportunity to publish it in the Creative Compendium pages of Grapevine, Lampeter's monthly newsletter. In bringing together *Tales From A Mountain Farm* this poem has been the only challenge to my editorship. While I insisted on its inclusion, Patrick considers it not to be a true tale from his mountain farm and therefore does not belong. I persisted, he resisted, until our happy compromise to separate it from the main body of work and slip it into my foreword. But while its position may have come about by compromise, it seems to me to be most fitting and thereby hangs a tale.

Without Regrets

I don't recall how it all began,
From squawking babe to tired old man ---
I remember walks, going out with Mam
In a flowery hat and a rickety pram,
I remember where we stopped and played
Under the trees in a woodland glade ---
I suppose I must have been nearly three
By the oak, the ash and the rowan tree.

I never was much of a scholar in school ---
The staff had me down as a right young fool.
They gave us a course on 'The Shakespeare Play',
Macbeth was the text one particular day.
I was kept in late for inattention.
It wasn't true, and I didn't mention
That I was away with the witches three
To the oak, the ash and the rowan tree.

→

The idlest boys grow to be men,
I had my moments, now and then.
The girl next door had eyes like sloes,
Our passions raced beneath our clothes,
So we ran to the woods like mad March hare
And under the trees we stripped off bare
With no one to tell on she or me
But the oak, the ash and the rowan tree.

To the wildest youth about the town
The time soon comes to settle down ---
My hands were hard and my back was strong
So I worked in the fields all day long,
But with harvest home and the ploughing done,
There was time to relax in the autumn sun
With a child sitting on either knee
By the oak, the ash and the rowan tree.

But now they've gone, the fledglings flown,
And me? I'm left to grow old alone.
I've had so much --- what can I give
To show the world I once did live?
I'll take a spade and I'll turn a sod
For the greater glory of man and god
And plant a crop I'll never see
An oak, an ash and a rowan tree.

I can't say I exactly know
Where, when or how I'll come to go.
But go I must, without regrets
And without a priest to hedge my bets.
'Neath an April sky or a harvest moon
My time's coming, late or soon,
The time to let my soul go free
To the oak, the ash and the rowan tree.

Introduction by Ifor Thomas

I am so impressed by *Tales From A Mountain Farm,* it has a place in the canon of great nature poetry books. Unlike RS (Thomas), who can only observe his "peasant" never getting under his skin, Patrick Dobbs is one of them, he is a "peasant", he writes from observation and experience. It reminds me of the simplicity and directness of W H Davies. But it's also laugh-out-loud funny, in fact the humour almost catches you out, as if he builds up a serious subject, lulls the reader in and then squirts him with water from a flower on the lapel of his tweed coat. I'm conflicted, I suppose, I've known Patrick for many years and admire him greatly. His unquenchable zest for life, whilst recognising that, inevitably, the end is getting closer, has been a constant source of inspiration. He has in this book of poetry captured a time that has now passed. He chronicles the life of a hill sheep farmer over almost sixty years in the beautiful but unforgiving landscape of Llyn y Fan. But Patrick is not a sentimental man, the winning vegetables in the annual show are magnificent, but tasteless, the beautiful pastries, stale. The sharp farmer's eye peering out from under that craggy brow misses nothing. The characters he describes are fellow farmers he has known, his own tribe, not some strange species to be observed from a distance. There is wonder to be found in weeds, bumbling badgers, he debunks myths and despises rules and authority.

But what shines through this book is his humour, sometimes black, sometimes self-deprecating, sometimes even slapstick. Even his last thought is to remind somebody to feed the cats. Patrick's life-style is unique and vanishing, this book is a chance to share his wonderment, to feel the wind of change blowing over the hills that will always be the same. Even the stones have beauty, even the storm can make you smile. To read these poems is to know that even though times and mores change, truth and humour will always endure. This book, it deserves to be a publishing success but being poetry, one never knows.

The Long Walk to Freedom

About a mile, and took some fifteen minutes,
The daily walk from school to railway station.
A canny run could get you there in ten,
An idling boy could take as much as twenty.
The problem was we weren't supposed to run.
Idling, like whistling, was frowned upon.

At last the last and happiest day arrived,
My last walk down that well remembered mile.
That afternoon the big man talked to us ---
Said how we must be sad to leave the place,
The focus of our lives, our work, our play.
He had some style, I will say that for him.

I'd thought he was a cut above the rest ---
His stance erect and magisterial,
He always wore a suit, and had a way
Of looking dignified and masterful,
Oozing authority and competence.
He stalked around as if he owned the place.

But when he stood in front of us and said,
"You must be feeling sad on your last day
And apprehensive of what is to come."
All the respect he had accumulated
Withered on the instant. Dead.
He was no wiser than the rest of them.

→

I well remember as I walked away
I made a point of never glancing back.
Now I could run or idle as I pleased,
Stick hands in pockets, dress just as I liked,
Use my school tie to keep my trousers up
And send my blazer to a jumble sale.

Life, real Life, my life could now begin.
The world was at my feet, joy in my heart
As I trod down that road for the last time
And whistled as I went my favourite tune ---
"Can you tell me if any there be
Who can give me employ
To plough and sow, and reap and mow,
And be a farmer's boy"

Flowers of the Fields

Daisy
Buttercup
Primrose
Bluebell
Daffodil
And Rose.

I loved those cows ---
So placid and amenable.
It is some thirty years since I last sat,
Bucket between my knees, a three legged stool,
And felt the throbbing surge of fresh made milk
Pass down a teat and froth into a pail.
I loved them all, with all their little ways,
The awkward ones who'd kick and skip about,
The quiet ones you didn't need to tie.

A solitary youth, I learned the job
From farmer Murphy and at Waterhatch.
In summer time a quick and easy chore,
On winter mornings by an oil lamp
And candles stuck into the window ledge.
First fetched them in and chained each in her place,
Then scrubbed and slooshed the standings afterwards.
But very soon I'd do the proper job ---
Just wet my hand, entice the milk to flow.
My bucket soon was full, with once or twice
A sideways squirt to please the cowshed cat.

→

It's all electric now, pipelines, robots,
Improvements all the way, less drudgery,
Output is up and wages up with it.
But at a cost, there are things we have lost ---
The rhythm of the days, the starlit nights,
A sense of oneness with the fields and woods,
The farmyard animals, the flowery names ---

Daisy
Buttercup
Primrose
Bluebell
Daffodil
And Rose.

The Colour of the Wheat

The colour of the wheat. My wandering years
When work was play and every day was work.
It was a time of hope when I forsook the hills
For Suffolk, Leicestershire and Lincolnshire,
A month in one place, two weeks in the next.

While wheat was green, with just a hint of blue,
I knew there was a little time to go
To earn some pennies hoeing sugar beet
Or pulling weeds from the potato field
Before the harvest trailers were brought out,
The combines greased, the tractors tuned to go,
The bailers serviced, the straw barns prepared.
Those dreadful sacks, four bushels and then some,
Two hundredweight at least to break your back
Waiting in piles upon the granary floor.
Wheat spoke of money, good and gutsy ground,
A different world from where I learnt my trade.
The ears filled out, the sun turned green to gold.
The gold was not for us, we got the chaff,
Moved on, a pittance saved, then moved again.

Eventually I bought my little farm.
No good and gutsy ground for me,
But mountain sheep, tough ponies, hardy cattle.
I don't regret the wandering years at all,
Remember without rancour those rich farms,
The huge machines and the four bushel sacks,
The colour of the wheat.

Sundays

"God made the Indians," John said to us
One Sunday afternoon on Wally's ranch,
Then added, "God made the White Man too."
That we agreed. It was beyond dispute.
But logic posed a dire consequence,
"The half-breeds, God never created them.
They're the Devil's children, Devil's doing."

The Sunday sermon over, we gulped down
Our coffee in the bunkhouse, went outside
To sit and watch the sun go slowly down,
The three of us, myself and Jens the Dane
And John from somewhere in Saskatchewan.
I liked the man. He knew an awful lot
About the ways of muskrats, antelope,
The flight of geese, the haunts of duck and deer.
He had seen buffalo and talked of bears,
Could rope a steer and bring him to the ground.
And he was tough. He worked from dawn till dusk,
Six days a week, with scarce an hour off.

But Sundays they were different. "I do
Hate Sundays, Sundays worst of all."
"Why's that?" I asked, "today we get a rest,
Sit in the sunshine. You can have a smoke."
"But then I get to think about my wife
And kids living in North Saskatchewan."
He'd leave them there for weeks, for months on end,
So he could work for money in the South
Here on this cattle ranch, Wells Ranching Company.

$\rightarrow$

And then I saw his family photograph ----
His wife, his children and their old grandma.
I realised at once just what he was ----
A half-breed from an Indian Reservation,
A devil child, not White nor Indian,
Lost to his tribe, but still not part of mine.

I'm sorry John, You surely must be dead ---
We had our chat some sixty years ago
And you weren't young and I am now quite old.
So did your children flourish in our world?
And do they cherish what remains of yours?
Believe me John, I learnt a lot from you
About much more than antelopes and bears,
And buffalo, geese, rats and ducks and deer.

Foxed

Abeyance

I saw my first dead fox in '43
Or was it 1944 perhaps.
I was a boy, but keen to show I could
Help harvest home as well as any man.
Two shires pulled the binder round the field,
The sails bent corn towards the cutter bar,
The knotter tied the sheaves and then we grabbed
Them, one in either hand, and stood them up
In clumps of six to make a sturdy stook.
Jim was the horseman, Ted stuck to his cows
But in the harvest field he drove the team
Perched high up on the binder's driving seat,
As Jim was recognised the better shot.
For as the horses trundled round and round
The rabbits, mice and rats, and pheasants too,
All creatures of the field, ran to hide
In what was still left standing of the crop,
But in the end they had to run for it.
"He's there," yelled Ted, "I see'd 'un, there 'e goes,
What shall we do? He's there --- the old dog fox."
What would we do? The hounds were shut in kennel.
The poultry fund was dry. The war was on.
But shoot a fox? Who'd heard of such a thing?
Dada Edmunds, dad to Jim and Ted,
A hunt committee member, he'd decide.
He didn't hesitate, "The way things are
I'd say we'd better kill 'im while we're here.
Hounds will come back when this war is won."

$\rightarrow$

And so it was, they did what is Not Done.
Jim shot the fox, and twenty rabbits too.
I took my pay, paunched ready for the pot,
A proud boy, and a wiser one I'd say.
I won't forget the day they shot the fox.

Revival

I first saw hounds in 1948.
Helping Frank Freeman feed his milking cows ---
We heard them first, the loud tumultuous cry
Of twenty couple on a burning scent.
Then here they were, all round us in a bunch,
Sterns up and noses down to catch the line
Lost for some minutes in some cattle foil.
Up comes the Master, Captain Ronnie Wallace,
Watches them a moment, knows at once
His fox will set his mask for Spoonley Wood.
A short note on his horn, hounds rush to him,
He casts ahead, hounds feather to the line
Then tumble over Freeman's boundary wall
And off they go again, "Has that big earth
Been stopped? I haven't seen the terrier man,"
Says Frank. And then the field comes full tilt,
Their horses clipped, manes plaited, fit to race,
Red coat, silk hat, white breeches, polished boots,
Crested brass buttons, quite a carnival,
Ladies riding side-saddle, young girls
Astride, then wiry men in ratcatcher
Who look as if they've got a horse to sell.
A pair of stragglers follow after them,
Then all are gone. Our world is quiet again.

→

Conclusion

While driving home from Oxfordshire one day,
In 1978, I passed right by
A spot that stirred a dormant memory
Of hounds and hunt staff trotting down the lane.
And what's there now? A pair of traffic lights,
A garish road sign and a string of cars,
A supermarket with its parking place.
I'd visited Les West, a childhood friend,
Who worked in stables when he was fourteen
As under ploughman with a team of shires.
"I have retired now," he said, "And my last job
Was tractor driving, music in the cab,
With air conditioning, and radio
Contact with our salaried manager.
Oh yes, there's shooting now, a pheasant shoot,
They pay for it, a hundred pounds a day,
The boss don't want no foxhounds round this way."
"I'll fares the land to hastening ills a prey,
Where wealth accumulates and men decay." [1]
Is that the message? Would I better say
"He cared not for that text a plucked hen
That saith that hunters be not holy men." [2]
It lingered on for twenty years or so,
A tawdry parody of what it was.
The plaited hunter now a half clipped cob,
The modern version of foxhunting dress
A plastic coat and rubber riding boots,
Familiar coverts just a second home
For distant cousins of an urban fox.
Old Chaucer's chickens came to roost at last,
And Goldsmith's village is commuter land.

1   *Oliver Goldsmith   The deserted village.*
2   *Geoffrey Chaucer Tales of Canterbury The Monk.*

Shearing

Just forty in the shed, twice that outside
Waiting in the yard to follow them,
Three hundred plus beside that in the field
Brought off the mountain yesterday.

I trip the gate into the catching pen.
Curl my right arm firmly round her neck.
She rises to her hind legs, close to me,
Then staggers back and slithers to the floor.

I love this job, the aches and pains of it,
A symphony of rhythm, sweat and muscle,
The yearly test of fitness, guts and skill.
One farming task defying automation.

I hold her firmly, tight against my thighs,
Reach for the clippers, make a pair of cuts
Down from her breast bone, quickly up her neck.
Move in a flash from chest right to her chin.

It was now very many years ago,
While working in the yards in Canada,
I saw an advert in the farming press,
'Sheep shearing courses. Scotland, Near Dunkeld.'

Another two swift strokes, her head held back
So no loose skin is caught between the cutters,
And then two more down to her shoulder joint
To make quite sure her neck is clean and bare.

→

And so I left my cattle droving job
To sail by cargo boat from Montreal.
Arrived in Bristol, travelled on by thumb,
And signed up with the Lister shearing team.

Now for her ribs and belly, here's the test,
If she's not fit, the grease close to her skin,
She won't clip out as tidy as she should.
If there's a slow bit this is where she'll be.

Godfrey Bowen, he's the father of it.
I saw the man in 1956
In Ashford livestock market, demonstrating
How he sheared the wool, controlled the sheep.

Watch how I'm going deep inside her groin,
A reckless move could amputate her tits.
Now to the tail, what a worthless bit!
More trouble than it's worth, but must be done.

Built like a wrestler he was, that tough
New Zealander, all brawn and brain.
He understood ovine anatomy
And showed the world what brains and brawn can do.

Now down her right hind leg and up her flank,
Two short strokes, then three much longer ones.
Be sure to get the third across her spine.
Clip round her head. Be careful of her ears.

→

So many shearers make a sport of this,
Compete for competence in style and speed,
But for myself I've work enough to do
Without trying to prove I am the best.

Her head between my knees, keep her skin tight
To clear her shoulder. Quickly down her flank.
Let her head loose, and bend across her now
To finish with a sweep to shear her leg.

How long did that take me? Think I was fast?
You should have seen that damn New Zealander!

Friends

I think of them as friends, not family,
And certainly not 'pets', but they are way beyond
A simple asset on a balance sheet.
So many now, a litany of names,
Spot, Flash and Sparkey, Toby 1,
Henry and Snowy, Megan, Nell,
Then Bell and Snowdrop, Tegwen, Timmy too
And more again, most good, some very good,
All dead, but still alive inside my head.

Roy was the first, unregistered he was,
Bought him off Bramwell, wizard of Garnwen,
For eighteen pounds in 1961.
A thickset dog, black coat, white mottled feet,
A friendly fellow and a worker too.
I rode a strong cob, Polly, in those days.
Once we found an awkward ewe alone
On Mynydd Myddfai by the forest fence.
He cornered her so I could lift her up
And sit her on my lap and trundle home ---
As often Roy himself would take a ride.

I soon decided one was not enough ---
What if he had an accident or died?
And so came Moss, a lean and agile sort,
More highly strung than Roy, but what a dog!
I started running in the trials then ---
Such times we had! We never travelled far
For years ago there was a sheepdog trial
In every other parish in these parts.

$\rightarrow$

I was so lucky with the dogs I had.
They'd quickly learn to push sheep through the pens,
To load a trailer, hold a lambing ewe.
But most I loved the unfenced mountainsides,
To see a dog drive stray sheep from my patch
Then bring my own ewes from far, far away
And pick out those I wanted from the bunch.
They had their different styles, special skills.
Bob enjoyed trials, Wimp preferred the pens,
Bluey and Solo entertained the kids.

Each had a little hut inside a run ---
Some kept a tidy house, and some did not,
But all so loved the place that was their own.
They lived for work, and when they got too old
For it they mostly had a year or two
To potter round the fields, guard the yard.
When life became a burden, without joy,
I'd see to it they did not suffer long.

And now I'm left with Ben (or Toby 11),
Fourteen years old, but still happy enough.
And Siân, mother of thirty six, playmate,
Companion, children's treasured favourite.
And their son Flik ---how keen and fit he is ---
The latest and the last one of his line.
We've had good times, and they were friends to me,
My fortune was to have their company.

Competitive Farming

The hedge layer, the guy who shears the sheep,
The ploughman and the sheepdog handler ---
They mostly learnt their trade while still in school.
A job yes, but a recreation too,
The ploughing match, the shearing competition,
The sheepdog trial --- each one to their own ---
A knack passed on, as much an art as craft.
Not just a living, more a part of life.
But who will follow in their footsteps now?
For will precision farming make their skills
Irrelevant as cavalry to war
Or archery to dealing with a fox?
Now GPS to measure NPK
And EID to trace a missing ewe,
Robotic cultivations, AMS
For dairy cattle fed DCPF,
Smart 'phones, computers, aerial photographs,
That's how they farm their fields, feed their stock.
Will ploughing true and straight, working a dog,
Shearing a sheep and laying down a hedge
Be some nostalgic rural heritage,
A quaint survival from a bygone age?
Perhaps a way of passing the weekend,
A countryside alternative to golf?
If I were born again, again fourteen,
Would farming weave its spell upon me still?

Sam Lee

A strip of grass on sandy ground
Between the Sunrise Industrial Estate
And the low-budget executive housing,
Blue-tinged, spiky grass, grass without future,
Soon to be car-park, slip road or squash court,
And here, in this unlikely refuge,
Sam's horse, Sam's last horse.
He looks almost as old as Sam.
"A Blagden," Sam told me proudly,
"Full Blagden"
A white mark, the mark of the Shire,
Marks that old warrior,
Sam's horse.

Where are you, Sam Lee?
On the Morfa, by the sea,
Between the houses and the shore,
On land, but not dry land,
Just a tiny plot on the very edge
Of our big world.

A plot allocated, grudgingly,
To keep you from roadside and lay-byes,
Commons and Open Spaces.
We have taken your stopping places.
This is your last stop.
You stop here.

→

Sam,
With your tales of hawking and tinkering,
Your radiators, refrigerators and radios.
You have an eye for it,
An eye for the copper, the lead and the brass.
But now your metallurgy,
Forged in your own folk history,
Has stranded you here
On the Morfa.

We have slept, you and I,
At different times, under the same hedge.
We've done business together
In horses and carts ---
The price of a bale of hay for a rusty hame.
We neither of us really belong here ---
We have a shared heritage, a long history,
That is neither English nor Welsh.

Be a proud man, Sam Lee.
Push your trolley bravely through the supermarket.
Feed your horse on bread and potatoes.
Prime your gamecock with nuts and raisins.
Beat base metal into magic charms,
Copper into amulets,
Old iron to burnished silver.

We cower beneath our bedcovers from the moon
But we cannot turn the tide.
We are stoic driftwood on a callous shore.
Yet when the rattle truck comes for the horse
And your last fire burns between land and sea,
My eyes, too old and dry for tears,
Will cry again.

Lampeter

Mostly I remember Lampeter
As somewhere on the way to somewhere else ---
Taking my kids out swimming in the sea
Or off to Dolgellau to buy hardy rams,
Or see my ewes grazing near Aberaeron,
Or going sheepdog trialling up the coast,
Or taking Welsh Black heifers to Tregaron
And night time nightmare trips to Holyhead
In stock wagons to meet the cattle boat
That sailed from Dublin on the evening tide.
How long it was --- Llangadog to Llanwrda,
Crugybar and Pumpsaint to Cwmanne.
Through Lampeter, a hiccup on my way
Then on again for hours and hours,
The Helter Skelter countryside of Wales.
Just passing through, with never time to stop.

And then one evening I did just that ---
And found, by chance, another Lampeter,
A bunch of poets in a study group
Whose talk was not of weather but of words,
Where lamb prices were quite irrelevant.
So strange they are, they have a private world
Of lecturers and school teachers and such,
Well versed in the fine arts, sophisticates.
And me? I go. I listen. Try to learn
From those who take their holidays in Spain
And think that everybody knows the names
Of wines, and foods such people like to eat.
Sometimes I say something, and comment on
This poem or that, but mostly I remain
A curious spectator, quiet about
The work of Martin, Derek, Jane or Sue.
I'm not, nor ever will be, *un ohonyn nhw*.[1]

       1...........one of them.

In Praise of Gramineae

Where would we be without the gramineae
The most successful plants found on the planet?
In rainforest or tundra, hot savannah,
Arid mountain country, lowland bog,
Fertile pasture, stony gravel bed,
A tropical lagoon or rocky cliff
Whatever else might grow there's always grass.
You cannot keep it down. Ask anyone
A martyr to their lawn all summer long,
Mow it today it grows again tomorrow.
When drought and sunshine desiccate a sward
Burn off the top and fresh young shoots appear.
Do they dispute the laws of botany?
The grasses have their own reply to that ---
Their special intercalary meristem
That makes a cut their cue to come again.
They multiply themselves by seeds of course
But spread unseen by wandering shoots as well ---
The subterranean subterfuge of couch,
Choker of crops, harbinger of despair.
In desperation you can dig it up ---
But never cut a rhizome with a spade
Or slice it with a harrow or a plough
For that's the way to propagate the stuff.

But for the most part, ninety nine percent
And more, the gramineae are friends to us.
All cereal crops are grasses for a start ---
The wheat that makes the flour to bake a cake,
A loaf of bread, a biscuit or a pie.
Rye that puts the vita in Ryvita
And puts the punch into rye whiskey too.
Then barley does what barley always does   →

Gets with some hops to brew good bitter beer.
Grow oats for porridge. What an honest dish
For working folk who live good wholesome lives!
(Don't speak to me of sowing wild oats,
And if you do don't bring the harvest home).
Maize, in the USA they call it corn,
Can make good whiskey too, and many folk
Depend on it to feed their family.
But first and foremost in the catalogue
Of fibrous staples from the grains of grass
Must surely be that joy of prince and peasant,
King of things savoury and queen of puds,
The greatest gift of all --- the gift of rice.

The sugar cane, perhaps the mightiest grass,
Will always be for me a crop of ill-repute,
A memory of slaves, of unmanned men,
And Indian indentured labourers
In fields of hardship, poverty and pain.
But it has many uses. Ethanol,
The fuel of the future (well perhaps),
And that sweet, heady distillate called rum,
And chopped up cane to feed to mules and cows.
Our flocks and herds? Wherever would they be
Without the family of gramineae?
In summer pastures they can safely graze,
And when cruel winter cuts the season's growth
The hay and silage fills the hungry gap.
There's oats for horses, wheat for hens and geese
There's barley ground up fine for fattening pigs
While sheep and cattle get compounded feeds.

→

They keep us warm and dry, the leaves and stalks.
Wheat straw --- what better than a well thatched roof?
Perhaps an Amerindian June grass one.
Want entertainment? Play a bamboo pipe
Sitting in comfort on a bamboo chair
Beside a pot of pampas grass.
Or play a game of croquet on the lawn
Or watch the racing on the sacred turf
Of Aintree, Epsom or Newmarket Heath.
Or are the golfers greens more like your thing,
The grass of Wimbledon or Twickenham?
So let us praise all grasses --- gramineae ---
The friend and saviour of all living things.
"All flesh is grass", the good book tells us so,
Isaiah, chapter twenty, see verse six.

Disconnect

I see them from the window of a train ----
The high rise flats in concrete jungle land,
The rows of houses built too close together.
They make me feel uneasy. Sad.

What kind of lives, I wonder, do they lead
Those families? The children most of all?
Within that man made world where do they see
That every creature born to live must die?

Have they ever picked a blackberry?
Touched the sweet velvet of a bitter sloe
Or gathered mushrooms before breakfast time?
Where do they find a fallen branch to burn?

Do they climb trees, or dam a tumbling brook
To learn the ways of waterfowl and fish?
And do they understand the wiles of weasels,
Know where the badgers live, the haunts of hares?

Through all those urban lights can they discern
The constellations of the stars at night?
Does dawn determine when they start each day?
Sunset forecast the task they face tomorrow?

Have they been witness to the pain of birth,
The bond between a mother and her young?
And have they seen the fade of faculties,
The inevitable closing down of death?

I see them from the window of a train ----
The high rise flats in concrete jungle land,
The rows of houses built too close together.
They make me feel uneasy. Sad.

The Tale of the Parish Cup

With hay safe in the barn, and winter still
To come, in those dog days of summer we
All had the chance to prove our prowess in
The Parish Cup on Bedwhirion fields.
Maldwyn Panthowell organised the thing,
Gwyn Nantgwynne lent a hand as well,
He'd done it annually since who knows when.
And in the end we held the trial there.

We'd clear the ground, set up a simple course,
Two hurdles marked the fetch, a Maltese cross
Would test the style of each shepherds' dog,
A narrow race to demonstrate control
And finally a small three sided pen
Completed, if you got that far, your run.
At the far end a Thomas boy put out
The sheep, three ewes each time, and how we hoped
To get a steady bunch that handled well,
Quiet, responsive, neither wild nor slow!

We'd find a judge, an outsider of course,
From Breconshire perhaps, or Cardigan,
And Tommy Bryn would keep the entry book
And watch his stop-watch with a buzzard eye ---
Nine minutes was the time that was allowed.
We mostly had a go, old note books would
Record their names, a Parish register ---
Dai Twm Nantyrodyn, Morgan Price of course,
His brother Wil the grid, and Gelligron,
Emrys Tymawr and Dai Pwllcalch were there,
Ieu' Acheth, Eddie Wenallt, Idris Hope,
Jo Gelli, Eric Morgan from Coedmawr ---
Ben Williams from Gorsddu once had a try
He cursed his luck, "My dog works well at home."

→

Then there were experts, Morgan Neuadd Fach,
And Llew Blaensawdde always had a chance,
Dai Henbont, he was pretty good as well,
And Cliff Cwmsawdde with his big red dogs.
We had our champions too, whose names were known
Far wider than the confines of our *milltir sgwâr*.
They made it look so easy, Glyn Penrhiw,
His brother from Cilgerddan, quite as good ---
Fortunately they were kind as well,
They kept their best dogs for far stiffer tests
To give us all a fair shot at the Cup.

But what's become of it? Where is the Cup?
We finished with the trial years ago.
We couldn't carry on. Some shepherds now
Just race over the mountain on their quads
And dogs do little more than dash across
From one bike to the other, hustle sheep
Along, can't sort them on the hill at all ---
Want one or two, they have to fetch the lot.
Then one man grazed two hundred ewes at most
But now their children, grandchildren more like,
Have nearer thousands, and their half-trained dogs
Could no more coax sheep round a trial course
Than drive a car or use a mobile phone.
Professional dog handlers now try
To make a living from what once was fun,
And half the people round the trials today
Do not keep dogs to look after their sheep
But keep some sheep to sharpen up their dogs.
They're good, there's no denying it, but how
Serious they are, they count their points
Like cattle dealers watch the price of beef.
The seasons turn, the failing autumn weather
Anticipates the winter storms to come,
Our summer's going, our dog days are done,
And something good has disappeared for ever.

The News

Middle East is on fire.
Afghanistan flares up anew.
Africa is on the brink.
Stock Markets collapse.
It is wet, cold and windy,
With a prospect of snow.
Rainwater drips from the bathroom ceiling,
Again.
My sheep need feeding by the mountain fence.
I must see to it,
Now.

The Boundary

1986

"Mr Davies? Sut mae Mr Davies? Beth am y boundary?
The sheep are getting through again............
We'd better do a good job this time. Do it tidy eh?............
Oes stakes 'da chi?........A wire?.......Mae wire gyda fi........
Pryd?...............Y fory te......tomorrow. Yn y prynhawn? In
the afternoon?..............
Ie. Ie."

It's two o'clock.
He brings the stakes, I bring the wire.
For five and twenty years our boundary's been here,
Two decades and a half, a quarter century,
Yes, I'd say it is, put any way you like,
A goodish part of any person's life.

We don't talk much, do Willie Bach and me.
We wave on passing when I go to town.
On Tuesdays, three or four times in the year,
We eye each other's fat lambs in the mart.
We swap the occasional stray ewe.
We have touched trolleys in the grocery,
And in the year the big snow came
I fetched his food supplies ----
Four tins of beans and two loaves of sliced bread.
In '76, the year we had the drought,
We did agree the pasture burned up bad.
Today we work, together, on the boundary.

→

We get to work.
He cuts the brambles, I take down old wire,
He's handier with a bill-hook than I am.
I free the rusty staples, coil worn barb,
And now, we've no escape, decision time,
We must determine where our fence will run.
In years gone by our boundary was hedged,
A line of hazel, sallys, ash and quick.
It followed nature's trail, not ours,
But posts and wire, that's another thing,
That runs where we decide to put the stakes.
To make it strong, with straining posts and struts,
It needs to be as straight as we can make it,
The wire tight enough to pluck a note
And all the stakes lined up like soldiers on parade ---
Look down the line, see one --- you've seen them all.

I like to offer him a bit of my ground first,
A yard, perhaps four feet, will be enough.
More would be profligate, less might seem mean.
A yard is roughly right, I'll never miss
A yard of mountain grazing, that's not much,
I'll get it back, and more, when I take some of his
To circumvent the rock above the bridge.
Do diplomats negotiate like this?
A gesture made, an offer taken up?
We hardly speak, we deal in fellowship,
Our boundary is much too sensitive
For any words, his words or mine.
Now dig. The two of us. Still strong and fit
Though he and I are now past our half time.
Age makes men crafty. This post hole is dug
With half the effort of our fresh, green, youth.
It's how we swing the shovel, aim the bar.

→

We work so hard we've not the breath for talk,
As suits two men of action, short on words.
But when we've gone two feet, with two to go,
We break our silence, we communicate.
The roots, y gwreiddiau, make our excuse.
"I'll get the bar," we always offer rather than suggest,
"And lever underneath them. See, fel yna."
He smashes with the shovel, cuts them off.
"Mae gwreiddiau yn bla, yn waeth na cerrig."
"Roots are a nuisance, worse than stones," he says.
It is agreed, that roots are worse than stones.
From roots and stones we work our way
Through cattle prices and the trade in ewes
To personal anecdotes, who once lived where,
How Welsh is seldom heard in Brecon now,
And "Aberaeron is a lovely town."

The hole is dug. The post goes in the ground.
We ram the earth around it with our boots.
He saws a notch, and I slot in a strut
Which stops the wires pulling out our post.
The hardest part is done. We break for tea.
I go to my house, he goes off to his.
I think of Brecon as a frontier town,
And Aberaeron, somewhere by the sea.
And people who once lived here, now passed on.
Today we worked, together, on our boundary.

Wil

2014

A quiet man, quite hard to get to know,
Neighbours for over half a century
And never once exchanged an angry word.
Not that we talked a lot over the years ----
A passing comment on the price of lambs,
Some idle gossip as we fixed the fence
That kept his sheep from mixing up with mine,
A brief phone call if cows were on the road
Or ewes had come down off the common land
Into his fields or to my holding pens.
He bought a bull from me decades ago,
A friendly one, that meant a lot to him.
And once when roads were blocked with drifted snow
I fetched his groceries from Mason's store.
I did not know his father very well ----
His English was no better than my Welsh
So chats with him were rather limited.
To tell the truth they seemed to find it hard
To get round all the work they had to do.
When he had gone Wil managed on his own
Until he married rather late in life.
His wife was not a country girl at heart
I never thought, and sadly she died young.
In 1968 he canvassed me
To vote against Sunday pub opening ----
I wonder who had put him up to it!
Wil never went too far away from home,
Not even to the village hall to hear
A local choir or to watch a film.
In recent years he tidied up his farm,
Trimmed hedges, fenced off trees and jobs like that ----
A good conclusion to a life of toil.
He died one morning as he lived, alone.
A quiet man, quite hard to get to know.

A Gander at Geese

They're good things, geese. I learnt a lot from them
When working on a farm in '53.
Last job at night, to shut them in, was mine.
"They bring the foxes," my boss used to say.
"Do they pay well?" I asked one afternoon.
"That's not the point. The question you should ask
Is *"Are they useful birds to have about? "*
I stood corrected. I could see they were.

If strangers came they made a fearsome cackle,
Stretched out their necks, advanced aggressively,
Wings flapping with beaks poised to pounce and peck.
That farm had few unwelcome visitors.
(In fact the Romans, they kept geese like that,
The Goddess Juno had a flock of them
That warned the garrison high on their holy hill
The Gauls had staged an ambush from behind.)

There's music in the names for breeds of geese ---
'Toulouse' and 'Embden' and the 'White Chinese.'
The 'Brecon Buff' remind me of a tale
Old people in Llanddeusant liked to tell
Of how the farmers gathered at the Cross
To race in pony traps to Brecon town
To drink, and spend, and drink at the Goose Fair.

I never fancied goose eggs much to eat,
Too rich, too oily, and in truth too big.
But geese themselves make quite a sumptuous dish
Roasted with lots of sage and onion stuffing,
Served with potatoes, sprouts and sausages.

$\rightarrow$

I'll skip the detail of killing geese ---
A pickaxe handle and a kitchen knife
Was all I'd need, and it was very quick.
The feathering of poultry is an art ---
Not everybody seems to master it
And for a year or two I did quite well
At Christmas time, for I could pluck and truss
A goose or turkey with the best of them.

They're greedy grazers, geese, and every one
Will scoff green grass as quickly as a sheep.
They need top quality and like it short,
With lots of clover and with dandelions.
A green goose, killed at Michaelmas, is best ---
Yes, better far than corn-fed Christmas geese,
For when they're full of wheat they grow too fat
So they are not so very nice to eat.

When I was small in wintertime I slept
Snug and cosy in a goose down bed.
Goose grease, that's fat to folk like you and me,
Was used in times gone by for many things ---
Rub on your chest to cure a cold or cough,
Rub on your joints to banish aches and pains,
Rub on your boots to keep them watertight
And roast potatoes in the grease of geese.

→

II

But when I think of geese my thoughts go back,
When, sixty years ago, a young man stood
In distant Demerara, by the shore,
And watched great flights of birds, their necks outstretched,
Wings beating out their pathway through the sky
In strict formation, like an arrowhead.
Their leader was the tip, the family followed,
Wave after wave of them skimming across
The Caribbean sea from North to South.

Where did they come from? That I cannot say.
The great plains of the USA? The Lakes?
Or further still, from Canada perhaps?
Where did they find their winter feeding grounds
Somewhere in Brazil? Or did they stop
In French Guiana or in Suriname?
Did they look for landmarks on the way
Or have a cranial compass as their guide?
A mystery that stirs me to this day.

III

In student days, in lecture rooms and labs,
I took a course in animal production.
We studied cattle, sheep and hens and pigs,
But geese were never on the syllabus.
If I was very rich, with cash to spare,
I would endow a University,
Sponsor research into the ways of geese,
Into their lifestyle and history.
A nobler field of study that would be
Than media studies, business management,
Creative writing or accountancy.
Our zest for knowing things must never cease
And we could learn an awful lot from geese.

Llanddeusant Community Hall
Neuadd Gymunedol Llanddeusant

Dathlu un mlynedd ar hugain.

Commissioned to celebrate 21 years since the purchase
of the old schoolroom by the community for community use.

You pass it, stranger speeding through,
Beside the road, grey, commonplace
And unremarkable.
A building overlooked,
Yet overlooking
Fields and trees
And farmsteads folded
In the folds of hills
Below the mountain crest
Of Bannau Sir Gar.
The school room once ---
Keeper of history and guardian of secrets
That these stone walls will never tell.
Where are they now, Rhiannon and Glyn,
Jane, Rosemary and John?
Have we, who come today,
Forgotten them?
And will we leave some tales of our own
When we too are forgotten?

→

"Aros mae'r mynyddoedd mawr
Rhuo trostynt mae y gwynt" [1]
The poet said, and added, to be sure,
"Mae cenhedlaeth wedi mynd
A chenhedlaeth wedi dod." [2]

Now is the time
To make some music of our own
Within these walls
And serve our generation as we can.
Step carefully ---
For we could be remembered
By the stones.

Ceiriog

1 'The great mountains stand
The roaring wind passes over them.'

2 'Generations have come
And generations have gone.'

Pigs

A somewhat apocryphal tale

Last autumn in Hereford market,
Beside poultry and sheep and some cows.
There really was quite a surfeit
Of suckling piglets and sows.

So I thought to myself 'here's a bargain',
They were healthy and sleek as could be,
Yes, I fancy myself as a pigman,
And the auctioneer sold them to me.

I built them a home in the garage
And fed them on buckets of food.
They gobbled potatoes and cabbage
Whenever they felt in the mood.

They rootled around in the rose-bed,
And dug up the vegetables too.
They demolished my neighbour's woodshed,
So I bought him another one --- new.

The fences and hedges they've damaged!
For pigs never can stand and wait ---
The lawn has been totally ravaged,
And there's nothing left of the gate.

They were fun when they came in the autumn,
When all in the litter were small,
But now I am sorry I bought 'em,
For I don't really like them at all.

So last Wednesday in Hereford market,
Seeing they'd grown to eight score,
I sold them.   And gosh, damn and darn it ---
I went and bought two dozen more.

Re-Wilding

A shiftless old farmer called Wilding
Decided to go for re-wilding
For it entered his head
He'd get more time in bed
If his land all went wild, thought Wilding.

The Elements

The elements are waiting at my door.
The kitchen stove my only company
As orange flames flare up inside the grate.
I look into the window, and I see
A framed self-portrait of an ageing face.
Beyond the pane, somewhere in the night,
My cattle huddle, hungry, hollow flanked
To shield each other from the winter blast.
Far on the slopes beyond the mountain gate
The sheep take shelter on the leeward side
Of every clump of gorse and shard of rock.
Each one of us is waiting for the day.

And I remember 1947.
I was a young boy then, and ranged the woods
As young boys do. In that deep labyrinth
Of trees with boughs and roots encased
In driven snow I came across a badger,
Frail and thin, pulling at a broken
Fleece still clinging to a long dead ewe.
We looked at one another, I walked on,
And he, perhaps too ill and old to care,
Resumed examining that putrid corpse.
The kitchen stove is good for airing coats
Still sodden from the day before.
I look into the window and I see
Between the branches of a chestnut tree
The ridge of Cefn Esgyrn, hill of bones.

→

And I remember 1963.
I was a young man then, and tough and hard
As young men are. I carried bales of hay,
One in each hand, and slung two bags of cow
Cake on my shoulders in a single load.
Sheep climbed huge snowdrifts over fences, gates,
To get from field to field, just as they wished.
I've got a faded photograph to prove it's true.
The kitchen stove is burning slowly now,
I need to fetch another load of logs.
I look into the window and I see
The farm outside is ready for the day.

The dawn has come at last.
I am an old man now, and worn and slow
As old men are. I take my coat,
Warmed nicely by the stove, put on my hat,
Go to the door, draw back the bolt,
And brave the elements.

White Winter

That first white winter was a shock to me ---
The pale faces drawn against the cold,
So worn and sad, so sunless and unsensual.
Why had I left the land of winter warmth?
Why had I left the one I left behind?
We met as strangers in the Punchbowl bar,
The steel band tinkling out calypso tunes
To make the fireflies dance and young blood race.
I sometimes feel she's still beside me now ---
Dark as creek water, silky smooth her skin,
Her hair as lustrous as an eagle's wing,
Her body soft and sweet as sugarcane.
We soared and tumbled while we had the chance,
Because we knew we were but birds of passage.
For those few months she gave me all she had
And in return I gave all I could spare.

And now I've lived with calculated love,
A suitable arrangement, sound, secure.
But sometimes, driving late on lonely nights
Or walking by myself across the fields,
I fantasize about what might have been.
What would I do if on one winter night
When snow has made the land a whiter white,
I had a timid knock upon my door,
Perhaps a letter or a telephone,
A shy enquiry --- Did I ever live
On a plantation on that distant shore
Across the Demerara from Georgetown?
Did I ever know an Indian girl?
To be precise, a girl called Meena Singh?
And I would know at once just who was there.
And I would give her everything I have
So she might give me all that she could spare.

The Show

A sequence of four poems commissioned to celebrate Llanddeusant show.

The Field

A dozen or so the evening before,
Fixing the livestock pens, roping the ring,
And on the day two hundred, maybe three.
There's all sorts here, the old and young,
Some new arrivals, some who went away
Returning on a visit to old haunts,
A passing stranger camping by the Cross
And summer residents, like migrant birds.
Most know each other, but not all are friends
For rivalries run deep, old scores don't settle.
But here, today, they wear a smiling face
To bless this field, our common stamping ground.
The far horizon, like a saucer's rim,
Contains us safe within our *milltir sgwâr.*
It's easy to escape, down country roads
And then a dash along the motorway,
But all of us have seen the sun chase mist
From the same morning meadows soaked in dew,
Have watched the kites and buzzards soar and swoop
Above familiar woods and farms whose names
Pencrug, Llwynpiod, Wenallt and Coedmawr
Mean more to us than Queens or Oxford Street,
The Palace at Versailles or Blackpool Tower.
This communal event, this stretch of earth,
The August afternoon --- these things we share.

Horticulture

Two vegetables of absurd dimensions ---
A pair of marrows.
Germinated precariously,   →

Planted with care,
Safeguarded from the frost,
Saved from the slugs,
Protected from the poultry,
Too large to cook,
Practically tasteless.
Completely useless ---
And absolutely magnificent.

Domestic

Cakes,
Flans,
Trifles,
Tarts,
Welsh cakes and scones
Competing with one another
In mouth watering exuberance.
--- Stale by tea time.

The Best Ram

Patted, poked and prodded.
Surrounded by knowledgeable men
Who've seen some good ones
In their time.

He stands in the sunshine
Panting slightly. Oblivious
To praise or criticism.

He chews the string
Tying the red card
To his pen,

Sniffs the evening air,
Catches a faint scent
Of yearling ewes ---
And thinks of autumn.

At the Railway Station

I watched her, blue-eyed, blonde and beautiful,
Set up her stall one Christmas time
While waiting for my son to meet me there
In Zurich. I was worn out from a day
Of trains and planes and now another train,
That world of flashing signs, recorded voices,
Check-ins, tickets, passports, boarding passes ---
And there she was, surrounded by her toys,
All wooden, carved by hand, a Noah's ark,
Some pecking hens, two woodsmen chopping logs,
A family of Russian dolls, some bears
That darted upwards when you pulled their strings,
A host of gnomes and elves, and frogs
And fishes, animals and birds. I think
I saw some people too, old men and ladies,
Little ones. A few were painted but
The best were not. All intricately carved
From ash and pine and sycamore and oak.
And she was there, the fairest of them all,
So young, so happy to display her wares.

I knew I had some minutes still to spare
Before he'd come and rustle me away.
We had a chat, the weather, Wales.
I asked her where she brought her carvings from,
Expecting her to name some alpine valley, far,
But not too far, from Zurich and the Christmas crowds.
"St Petersburg," she said.

$\rightarrow$

"Hi dad!" He came too soon, "I'll take your bag."
And so he took me in his charge again
As once, so long ago, I would take him.
We had no time to say a last goodbye.
And now I'm home again, with sheep to feed,
A fence to mend and firewood to stack.
And where, I sometimes wonder, is she now ---
St Petersburg?

Forgetfulness

He always was a big man in the mart.
He had a double decker trailer in the days
When most of us brought our sheep in a van.
He'd bring at least a score of lambs each week
And very often quite a good few more.
I never did know just where he came from ---
A small place I believe, near Nant yr Hwch,
On shallow soil way beyond Cilycwm.
But upland grass was never good enough
To feed up stock the way he managed to.
He rented fields, two dozen acres here,
A hundred somewhere else and sixty there.
He boasted once his sheep were spread about
From Haverfordwest to Hereford and then
From Aberystwyth down to Ammanford.
He was a happy man who loved his trade
And knew just how to pick and choose a lamb.
He had a piece of paper that told him
What price per pound of graded carcass weight
Would translate into so much pounds per head ---
We had no pocket calculators then!

It's quite a tedious job, is selling lambs ---
An early start to get them there and weighed,
A long wait for the grader to come round,
And then an hour or two to see them sold.
He helped us pass the time with doubtful tales
Of sheepdogs that he'd trained, and ponies too,
And how to catch fresh sewin with a gaff.

→

A jovial fellow with a cheery word
For everybody --- drover, auctioneer,
The buyers, fellow vendors, hangers on,
But mostly what he knew was where to find
A field, well fenced, well watered, good fresh grass
To get some lean lambs ready for the Mart.

I saw him last one Tuesday by the pens,
Joking that he had rented so much ground
He hardly knew which sheep were grazing where.
"I won't forget," he said, "I really must
Write it all down and mark it on a map.
If I drop dead ---who knows where they might be?"

He never came again. That Saturday
He didn't make it home from off the hill,
An accident, it seemed he slipped and fell.
His funeral was huge --- we all were there ---
And afterwards it seemed he had forgotten
To do what he had said he ought to do.
I sometimes wonder, as I drive around
And see some unmarked ewes with suckling lambs
If anybody ever found them all.
I make a resolution, there and then,
To wage a war against forgetfulness.

History

1991

My days begin squatting by a black cow. My black cow.
In thirty years I've gone through half a dozen cows.
All were black.

In winter, the crude shelter of the barn.
In summer, the open fields and the sky.
Sometimes blue.

I fumble for her teats in the hair of her udder,
I squeeze and pull, a rhythm develops,
And the bucket is full.

But the postman, the roadmen and the reservoir keeper,
They don't squat beside a black cow. Or any cow,
Of any colour.

When my cow and I have gone, as sometime we will go,
There will be no black cows in this barn, or these fields,
Anymore.

Will anyone squat beside a black cow and squeeze
Her udder in these parts, or anywhere,
Ever again?

Unnatural

When those first farmers grew a crop from seeds,
Stopped foraging the woods and wild savannah
To meet their family and village needs,
Were they told they were offending Allah?
"It is not right. It is unnatural."

And when they put their oxen to the plough
And made a share and coulter turn the sod,
Kept a few hens, some sheep, a fecund sow,
Were they breaking any law of God?
"It is not right. It is unnatural."

When we began to spray weeds in the fields
It soon was plain it would not take us long
To improve food quality, increase our yields.
Were we really doing something wrong?
"It is not right. It is unnatural."

Milk cows by robot? Spread the fertilizer
By GPS from satellites in space?
Give laying hens an air-conditioner?
Is farming falling now so far from grace?
"It is not right. It is unnatural."

Nature

Goodbye to hoe and sickle,
Hello to GM crops,
Mix up their genetics
Our progress never stops!
We fertilize our fields ---
How do we get it right?
We're told just where to put it
By a helpful satellite.
The sheep are getting scratchy?
Organophosphorous
Will sort them out quite quickly ---
Although it's bad for us.
Your cattle fatten slowly?
Stick hormones by their ear ---
If anyone asks questions
Just make them disappear.
It's clever to be able
To analyse a gene,
But who could have predicted
A dish washing machine?
We go sky high in spaceships,
We've landed on the moon.
Never met a Martian?
You might do very soon.
If we can split an atom
We can do anything ---
Don't worry about NATURE
That's an old fashioned thing.
Yet when someone flew over
The ruins of Chernobyl
The land he saw beneath him
Was green with chlorophyll ---
And what did so upset him,
To make him quake with fear?
Not radioactive debris
But wolves and elk and bear!

Day of Night

When I walk down through fields and woods
As dusk replaces daylight on the farm
It is a quiet time, and merciful.
The silence only broken by the owl
Who makes a home out of a hollow tree
And calls ----- Is that an owl? Or could it be
The passionate shrieking of a courting fox?
The squeaky bats are much harder to hear,
Their fluttering flight uncertain, ill defined.
The badgers will, I know, be coming out
To snuffle through the ferns and fallen leaves.
When sky is clear I see the North Pole star
That kept the Pharaoh's vessels on their course
And guided that misguided mariner
From Troy on his unlikely odyssey.

And I remember, standing in the lane,
A girl who came from Wigan, Lancashire,
Gazing in wonder at the night time sky.
"I've never seen so many stars before,"
She said, "Where I come from suburban lights
Make day of night, such stars invisible."
"Make day of night", an easy thing to do
Now we make light by pressing down a switch.
Should sunset circumscribe a working day?
Planes not take off and people stay at home?
Now industry and commerce never stops
And there's no refuge from the world of toil.
We made, by accident, some hell on earth
When we ignited flames of lasting light
And banished darkness from our lives for ever.

Dai John

Dai John, the blacksmith, made me a special bolt ---
He took the metal pin that held an old cart-wheel to the axle,
Hammered it to shape, then turned it on his lathe
To cut the spiralled groove that screwed it to the nut.

He took the iron band off the old wheel,
Split it into three, heated each end in his forge,
Then beat them on his anvil to make a rigid arc
That fitted --- exactly --- above my farmyard gate.

Dai John, convinced atheist, roused his neighbours
Each Sunday morning playing the organ, beautifully.
His tastes were sentimental --- *Danny Boy* and *Myfanwy*
Were his favourites --- and when the spirit moved him
He could get all Church Street humming *Calon Lan*
Or tapping their feet to *The Battle Hymn Of the
American Republic*.

He made a working model of James Watts' beam and
piston engine.
He'd never seen the original but copied it from a picture
In *The Boys' Book of Great Inventions*.
And when I praised him for his handiwork,
He said, "James Watt never had a picture --- or a book."

Dai John, the blacksmith, is dead. More recently
His wife died too. I saw his engine in a council skip,
And Church Street will never waken to his tunes again.
I mislaid the bolt he made for me some time ago,
And the arch above my gate will eventually be
Lying down amongst the nettles.

And when his friends, and mine, have all passed on,
No one will even know his name --- Dai John.

Homecoming

They make it home, the swallows and the swifts,
Reclaim their summer season in the barn,
Restore their battered refuge on the beams.
The bats, homecoming from their winter roost,
Reoccupy their perch beneath the slates.
Explain it if you can. Or tell me how
Atlantic salmon navigate the seas
To find the gravel bed where they were born,
And eels can wriggle on a wet commute
Three thousand miles to breed and back again?
Why does the horse I'm riding prick his ears
The moment that I turn his head for home?
How good to know that there are still some things,
Quite simple things, we cannot understand.

A470

The A470, it takes me down
To Cardiff, to an unfamiliar world
Of shopping precincts, towering blocks of flats,
Glass fronted offices and homes in rows
With garages and gardens facing front,
Where children play on roller skates, mothers
Push prams and old men sit in parks.
Streets teem with people, all intent it seems
On some important business of their own
That leaves no time to pass the time of day
With strangers like myself from far away.
Just sixty measured miles is all it is ---
Why does it feel like another planet?

One trip to Cardiff lingers in my mind.
I can't remember now just why I went,
But I met someone on my journey home,
A brief encounter that I can't forget.
I stopped near Pontypridd, left the main road
To call in at a branch of B & Q,
A temple to that cult called D.I.Y..
There were a few small things I had to fix ---
A wobbly doorknob and a tap that dripped,
A lampshade that was all awry and cracked.
I was directed to a quiet aisle
Where piles of lampshades cluttered every shelf.
A shopper caught my eye, well-dressed, refined,
A very proper lady, without doubt
Above my class. The thing that struck me most
Was that she was 'well–groomed', hands manicured,
Complexion soft, inviting as a rose.

→

Her outfit was, to borrow Shakespeare's lines,
Quite surely *"Costly as her purse can buy,*
But not expressed in fancy, rich, not gaudy."
All with the style of a thoroughbred
Prepared and ready for a bloodstock sale.

Business was quiet, we were there alone,
Taking our time to make a careful choice.
Then suddenly there was an accident
As scores of lampshades clattered to the floor,
Perhaps her hand slipped as she lifted one
And one dislodged another and so on.
Anyway of course I kneeled down
To help her pick them up and put them back.
"Do you live this way?" She asked me. "No I don't.
I come from Wales, beyond Storey Arms. And you?"
"I have a flat in Cardiff, near Roath Park."
We talked of lampshades, which would suit us best,
I wanted one of those round paper globes
While she fancied a red glass panelled one
To put over the light-bulb by her door.
We both stood up then went our separate ways,
Myself to plumbing and door furniture
And she to look for other things elsewhere.
But when we went to the checkout to pay
It chanced we were together in the queue.

Beside the entrance to the premises
A stall sold soft drinks, tea and cakes and stuff.
"Shall we have a cup of coffee?" I asked her.
"Why not," she said," I think I have the time."

→

She asked about my farm, the animals.
I took her through the seasons, one by one,
Lambing in springtime, summer shearing sheep,
And autumn taking fat lambs to the mart,
Then winter feeding cattle in the barn.
She thought it was hard work, but sounded fun.
She was surprised to learn I lived alone ---
And did I really ride round on a horse?
She was a listener, and flattered me
By showing interest in me, my life.
"And what about yourself, what do you do?"
"Me? I'm an escort, keeps me very busy."
She saw I looked perplexed --- explained to me,
"I go with men for money. Now I'm off,
There are a lot of calls I need to make."
She rose to leave. She kissed me on my cheek
And touched my hand --- then she was gone.

I looked down at our table and I saw
She'd left her small white business card.
"Mandy of Roath. All services," it said,
Above the number of her mobile phone.
I gathered up my things, went to my truck,
Drove slowly up the A470
To Storey Arms, left for Defynnog,
Through Sennybridge, Trecastle, turned to home.
I put my tap-washers, my paper shade,
The screws I'd bought, down by the kitchen sink.
I took her card and laid it on my desk.
It stayed there many months, well years in fact.
I never dialled her number, called her up.
Sometimes I think perhaps I should have done.

Forage

Each February I go foraging for fodder ---
To Hereford to buy some hay and straw.
An auctioneer brings out a catalogue
And I go round the farms to see each lot.
There might be five bays here, a hundred tonnes,
And just next door perhaps five hundred bales.
I know my job, I estimate the weight
And calculate how many lorry loads.
If I work out the distance from my farm,
Multiply that by price per loaded mile
It tells me just how much I dare to pay ---
Depending on the quality of course ---
Only the best for ewes and in-calf cows
But younger cattle thrive on coarser stuff.
It all depends on when the hay is cut,
The weather at the time, the type of grass,
The clover content and which weeds as well.
And there are other things to think about.
Is access good? Is help on hand to load?
How quickly must the vendor's barn be cleared?
Six weeks is fine, and six months better still,
But six short days is hardly time enough!
Now then of course I have to bid for it ---
And many buyers are as shrewd as me!
I never take a chance or buy unseen,
Mistakes can prove expensive, that's for sure.
I've gone to Hereford for fifty years.
I know the farms and all the farmers too,
Who you can trust and which ones to avoid.
But lately I have come to recognise
My past is long, my future rather short.
So all that effort, all that expertise,
Will just be something that has been --- and gone.

Grapes & Etcetera

All would be absolutely fine
If I had a huge grapevine,
A mango tree, some coconuts,
Cassava roots and monkey nuts,
A rooftop garden ripe with melons,
An orchard growing juicy lemons,
Bananas, paw paw, pineapples,
Oranges and custard apples.
It would even be quite nice
If I could grow a field of rice.

But in Llanddeusant we can never
Beat the wild and windy weather.
Some years there is just so much rain
All profit gets washed down the drain.
Any field of seeds we sow
Must withstand both ice and snow
And winters are so cold and wet
Stock breeding is our only bet.
In fact my fields are so steep
All I can raise are woolly sheep.

Rams

Get rams
Go North.
No Improved Welsh for me
Or woolly coated Cheviots with backs like blotting paper.
Sell me those hardy tups, all hair and horns,
The sort you see on Snowdon and North East of Corris
Where spring is late, the summer wet and short
And autumn just an interlude before
The winter, cold and grey and long.
It means an early start on sale days.
Get up by five and on the road by six
To start those weary miles of ups and downs
And twists and turns that just go on and on,
Llanwrda, Pumpsaint, Harford then Lampeter,
Talsarn, down to Llanrhystud near the coast,
Blaenplwyf and Chancery, Llanfarian,
Through Rhydyfelin to Llanbadarn Fawr
Branch left for Capel Dewi then Bow Street,
Pass Talybont and Taliesin and Tre'ddol,
To Furnace, Eglwys Fach, Glandyfi, now
It's Derwenlas, Machynlleth and up hill
To Ceinws, Corris. At Cross Foxes Inn
Turn left down to Dolgellau livestock mart.
I've got to know the road-signs, all the farms,
The garages and little village shops
Although I never stop along the way.
For I'm too keen to see what rams are there,
Then hurry home for I've got work to do
And stamp my mark on all my purchases.

$\rightarrow$

Worth the trip? To buy young mountain rams
Whose progeny will never meet the spec
Required by the supermarket trade,
Be ready for the world of ready meals?
Why would I want a flock of sheep like that?
What use are they? I'll tell you what they are.
They're rooted in the land from which they came ---
Once settled in they are as much a part
Of this, my farm, as are the rowan trees,
The gorse and whinberries, the woodpeckers,
The kingfishers and brown trout in the brook,
The water voles, the rabbits and the hares.
They stick around, survive the wildest weather,
Will still be here when you and I are gone.
They're tough, and mountainous, and Welsh.

Old Measure

Tell me a horse is standing sixteen hands
I know how tall he is --- I ought to do
I worked with them for seventy years or so.
But say to me he's that in centimetres
I've simply no idea what size he is.
But horse passports today are metric measure,
Not hands, just centimetres, one six two,
Or one six two point five to be precise.
And acres are all hectares nowadays ---
Now if I see a twenty acre field
I know how many cattle to put in.
But twenty hectares is a mystery,
I need my pocket calculator then.
And as for oxgangs, hides, virgates and such
Well they were just a bit before my time.
I do remember bushel measures though ---
Confusing really, apples, beans and oats
Take different weights to fill a bushel bag.
When I first worked for Freeman carting grain
We had four bushel sacks of wheat to load.
They are illegal now I'm glad to say ---
Catch them just right and they were hard to lift,
But catch them wrong and they would crick your back ---
So goodbye wages for a week or two.

→

On decimal day, in 1971,
When sixpences, half crowns and threepenny bits
And farthings were consigned to history,
It took some time for me to calculate
What three and four pence for a pound of sprouts
Would be in new pence for a kilogramme.
I must admit it made an easier task
To keep my books and do the farm accounts ---
A whole days' work took just an hour or so!
How many pints a litre, quarts to gallons?
And distances are disappearing fast ---
Seventy eight inches to a rod or pole or perch,
Then four rods to a chain, ten chains a furlong,
Eight furlongs to a mile. All racing folk
Remember that, and guineas too of course.
Where will it end, this rush to standardise,
To make us fall in line, be uniform?
Is there no room in this big world of ours
For quirkiness, for eccentricity?
For my part, for the bit of time I have
Before I too become an ancestor,
I'll stick with acres, guineas, quarts and pints,
With pounds and furlongs, hundredweights and hands.

Union

Now every time I gather in my flock
I thank my lucky stars I'm not a sheep,
Cajoled and bullied, chased around by dogs,
Pushed into folds and forced into a race.
And what comes next, they surely ask themselves,
Foul medicine forced roughly down their throats?
Feet trimmed while squatting on a concrete floor?
A hypodermic needle jabbed inside their leg?
Perhaps squeezed into that small catching pen
Before some uncouth shearer clips their coats.
Their mates found for them, never have a choice,
Their little ones all whisked away too soon,
Their tails cut off, and those unlucky boys
Castrated and dehorned --- no painkillers!
And sometimes loaded in a farmers' truck
To go off on a journey, who knows where?
It's time that sheep demanded basic rights,
Got organised, set up a picket line,
And built a powerful trade union.

Hands On

I always was a hands on man myself ---
I first went to the farm when I was nine,
Stooking the sheaves of corn, collecting cows
From field to shippon ready to be milked.
At twelve I learnt to milk by hand ---
No milking parlours with machines back then!
I humped the bales, lifted heavy sacks,
And sometimes drove a tractor down the lane.
First job from school was on a farm in Devon.
We spread the muck from heaps with a dung fork,
And I was champion at hoeing swedes.
Hay time and harvest I was always there,
Pitchfork in hand to build a tidy stack ---
Then scything rushes, splitting hazel spars,
To cover it with thatch against the rain.
I learnt my trade, and revelled in the work
Round England, Ireland and America,
Until at last I settled down in Wales,
Began to farm, hands on, a one man band.
Eventually I could hire help
But always I was there to set the pace,
To shear the sheep while others rolled the wool,
To take the toughest task, the hardest day.
But after fifty years of it and more
I've found that lifting rams or rolls of wire
Is not as easy as it used to be.
I've had to learn my hardest lesson yet ---
Be less hands on, to start to let things go,
To come to terms with what is possible.
The days get shorter, not too many left,
The night draws in, what does the evening hold
Before I go upstairs, turn off the light?

Wilson & Me

Wilson is dead, but I am just alive.
He passed through here a hundred years ago.
I saw his handiwork this afternoon ----
Four stones: one lying flat upon the ground,
Two standing vertical, one on each side,
And one across the top to make a roof.
A little tunnel about six inches square
Set deep into the soil of Trosnant.
How long it is, how far it goes,
I cannot tell, or even estimate.
It still discharges water to the ditch
I opened up near sixty years ago.

You and I, Wilson, have this in common.
We both have tried our best to drain this field
And turn it from marsh to pasture land,
Were briefly part of this community,
But just as birds of passage. You a Scot,
Myself a wanderer of no fixed abode,
We leave no descendants to inherit
Those skills and artefacts we honed and cherished.
We have been pioneers. More followed us ----
The transients who come, live here, then go
Like soldiers at the front in foreign wars
Who leave their mark but leave no kith or kin.

$\rightarrow$

Here history is drawing to a close ----
The generations that went on and on,
Made a continuous narrative of toil.
The young forsake the ways their parents knew,
A life in mud and muck and Wellingtons.
The ties of loyalty to tribe and trade
Disintegrate, longstanding family feuds
Abandoned, unresolved, irrelevant.
The school has closed, the roadside shop has gone,
Likewise the Post Office and Public House.
One chapel still remains, the Church still stands,
But only filled for feasts and funerals.

We are a Parish of the elderly ----
Retired folk whose working lives were spent
In offices, in schools, or hospitals,
A few redundant military men
And worn out farmers who hang grimly on
Because they are afraid of the alternative.
Old names become forgotten, Wil the Grid,
Dai Twm Nantyrodyn and Eric Coedmawr,
Ieu' Aceth, Ben Gorsddu and Glyn Penrhiw
Are now replaced by 'And Sons Ltd'
Or 'Us & Co'. Soon all of us will be
Forgettable, as Wilson is, and me.

Lake Lady

I've grazed my flock high on the mountainsides
Around the lake known as the Llyn y Fan
For close on sixty years. I know it well,
The rocks, the cliffs above, the floating flowers.
I've been there every season, time of day,
Often on foot, as often on a horse,
Always with dogs, sometimes with two or three
But sometimes only one. I look for sheep,
Moving them up and down, this way and that,
Drive strays away, coax mine along
Towards Fan Foel, the ancient walk
Their ancestors have grazed since time began.
I've gathered by the moon, in rain, in snow,
When wind has whipped up waves, when all is still,
In mist and sunshine, drought and freezing cold.
I've seen and felt the mountain's every mood.

On Sunday afternoons in summertime,
And nowadays in winter weather too,
The people come, in ones, in twos and threes,
In groups of ten or twelve, or maybe more.
They struggle up the track towards the Llyn
In outfits from an outdoor clothing store.
Sometimes I wish that they had not left home.
Do they expect to see a Lady rise,
The Lady of the Lake? Star of a tale
You're sure to find so aberrant and weird
You won't believe it if I write it down.

→

I will say this for her, she's just the thing
To swell the coffers of the tourist trade.
The National Park has even stuck a plaque
Beside the place where punters park their cars;
A brief synopsis, leaving details out,
Of how the farmer's boy seduced the girl
And took her off to share his life on earth.
They've even done some artwork of the lake,
The Lady wading to the stony shore,
Dark browns and blue, a touch of green and black.
I've read the script, and seen the picture there ---
Don't those fools know that she has yellow hair?

Last Harvest

The crops are cut, securely put away,
All ready for the worst of winter storms.
I stroll along, saucepan in hand, with Siân
The sheepdog bitch toddling close behind,
To gather our last harvest while there's time.
The blackberries are ready, rich and plump,
Swollen by rain and ripened by the sun.
I take the crook I used for handling sheep,
It comes in handy now for hooking briars
That bear the biggest berries, though it
Seems but yesterday that Siân and I
Were working up the mountain, on Fan Foel,
Gathering my flock down to the sorting pens.
There comes a time, a time to make some time
For what one time I had no time to do ---
Like walking hedgerows picking blackberries.

My pan is nearly full. Now one more thing ---
Stop in the garden by the apple tree
I planted fifty years or so ago.
They're hanging ready, shiny, ripe and plump.
A giant of a tree it has become,
I have to stretch, reach with my crook
To hook the branches, give them a good shake,
A horde of Bramleys cascade to the ground.
I gather them and take them to the house.
Tonight I'll sit down with a kitchen knife
Peeling the apples, cutting out the cores,
Add sugar, boil them up with blackberries.
My last harvest? That I cannot tell.

Mischance

I tell the truth, I don't deceive,
But here's a tale you won't believe.
I planned to cross the Atlantic Ocean,
And, being me, I had the notion
To travel cheap, on a bargain ticket,
Bought on the net at the last minute.
The Wales I left was white with frost,
I would have gone at any cost.
I made my way through ice and snow
To the airport at Heathrow,
I climbed on board, the plane took off,
But someone saw a wheel drop off.
I could not say how far we went
To make quite sure the fuel was spent,
For hours and hours we flew around
To get us safely back to ground.
Ambulances, blue lights flashing,
Made it plain we could be crashing,
Fire engines lined the runway
As we touched down, but I must say
Our pilot was a skilful chap
And got us down without mishap.
They hired another aeroplane
But we could not take off again,
The pilot had to take a rest.
And so the airline thought it best
To find another one, but he
Slipped on black ice he did not see,
Got from his car, and had a fall
And ended up in hospital.

$\rightarrow$

This was getting quite absurd,
Eventually they found a third.
We took off again at last,
We're on our way, and going fast,
A tail wind helping us along
It should not take so very long.
But then by damn, above Tobago,
A fuel gauge began to go.
It wouldn't work, we'd have to land ---
This was not the trip I'd planned.
We'd have to stay at least two nights
While they put the gauge to rights.
Did I complain? I had more sense ---
A posh hotel, at their expense,
A private room, a gentle breeze,
Parrots, iguanas in the trees,
A paradise of sand and sea
And waiters waitering on me.
It was indeed a marvellous thing,
Two days being pampered like a king!
But then, worse luck, the gauge was mended ---
My unplanned holiday was ended.

My Garden

"...... In Hawaii we don't control weeds. We eliminate them."
                Hawaiian pineapple growers' senior agronomist.

I neither mow nor cultivate my garden.
It is a Celtic rain-forest
Of perennial rye-grass,
Annual, smooth and rough stalked meadow grass,
Sweet vernal, cocksfoot, lop grass or soft brome,
The fescue family and Yorkshire fog,
Timothy, couch grass and a rogue black oat.

My garden is a playground for grasshoppers,
Caterpillars and less familiar insects ---
Green, blue and black,
Piebald and speckled, dappled, roan and rainbow,
Opaque and lustrous, gregarious or solitary,
Fliers, creepers, climbers, runners, jumpers or tunnellers
That tax the lexicon of entomology.

My garden has no flower-beds.
It has never been disturbed by the whine
Of Mickey Mouse machinery.
I never go to work in my garden
For it's a place of relaxation, contemplation, reflection
And study, as my horticultural skills
Have lost their competitive edge.

→

Come around my garden, where the comfrey
And dead nettles, shepherd's purse
And lady's bedstraw
Compete for space with St John's wort
And spleenwort, meadowsweet and dog's mercury,
Sow thistles, black nightshade
And purple rose bay willow herb.

There are apple trees in my garden,
Cookers and eaters, and three crabs
Brought home from Hereford in 1967.
A flowering cherry that flowered once in forty years,
A Norway spruce that came indoors
For every Christmas in the 70's
Rowan and elderberries to make wine,
And one horse chestnut --- candle and conker tree,
And blackcurrants, rhubarb and red gooseberry.

My garden could tell you tales ---
A quince from Christine,
A plant from Jean,
Monbretia from Alexa, Periwinkle from Cathleen,
Polyanthus in a broken pot from Nye ---
And that grey stone, the round one over there,
Retrieved, with passion, from Pwllheli on the Llŷn.

My garden is open to visitors.
Some fly in, bullfinch and chaffinch,
Swallows and house martins,
Racing pigeons on a stormy day,
And every spring a pair of courting doves
Arrive some dawn, and by dusk are gone ---
To leave me on my own, with bats.

→

Others are more cautious and pedestrian,
The hedgehog and the polecat,
Shrew and vole,
And in that ditch a colony of palmate newts
Keep company with leaping frogs and toads,
While from the field beyond a tired horse
Gazes wistfully at various varieties of vetch.

And in a broken barrel by the door a honeysuckle,
Stolen from the hedge,
And in the gateway
Mayweeds and plantains bind the gravel tight,
And in amongst the stones spring saxifrage and stonecrop,
And in Hawaii they don't control weeds either
--- They eliminate them.

Coed Tirbwch

As I walked through the badger's wood
I paused on my way home and stood
And sensed by sound and sight
The daytime passing into night.

The birds that brightened up my day,
Bullfinch and woodcock, pigeon, jay,
All gone. They'd vanished, just like that,
And in their place flit owl and bat.

Beyond the trees a mountain fox
Made for his den amongst the rocks,
While in their sett, deep underground,
Those bumbling badgers rummaged round.

I went across a field of hay
Fresh baled to carry yesterday
And ready now for next year's crops ---
That endless round that never stops.

But time is catching up on me,
What's gone is more than what will be,
And when my final audit's done
Will it conclude I lost --- or won?

Do my few fields better show
Than when I came here years ago?
I spread the lime, I sowed the seeds,
I drained the pasture, cut the weeds!

I'm not the man I might have been,
But I just hope it will be seen
That I made out as best I could,
And left the badgers in the wood.

Tale Of An Off-Road 4x4 Expert

I've been away, a whole week away,
So now I'm back there's work that must be done ---
Check post and messages, re-light the fire
And feed the sheep. They get hard blocks and hay.
The hay's no problem it goes by the gate,
But blocks I need to scatter far and wide.
I didn't fancy heaving them all out
From Land Rover to tractor, so I thought
I'd run them to Tirbwch along the track.
Elwyn Plasnewydd cut it out for me.
A dab hand with a digger Elwyn is,
Could lift a flowerpot off a windowsill
And put it down unbroken --- time on time.
He made it good, just wide enough it is
To take a tractor or my Land Rover.
It's served me very well for many years.

I use it often taking hay to stock
And stakes and wire for the mountain fence,
Collecting firewood, the odd dead sheep.
It snakes along, crosses the drainage ditch
I dug myself in 1962,
Over the stream where cattle huddle close
Below the rocks to shelter from the wind,
On by a most enormous badger sett,
And here's a tricky bit, it's safe enough
Except when leaves, washed down in wintertime
From oak and ash and alder high above,
Conceal the track --- for on the right hand side
A precipice, a truly fearsome drop.

→

Another stream, swing left amongst the trees.
Another ditch (I need to put a culvert here),
A steep pitch down to Nant y Creigiau
Then up and out into my flattest field.
An easy run on dry and sunny days,
But if it snows or frost freezes the track
Or even if it's swamped by heavy rain
Watch out. Proceed with caution.   Better still
Stay in the yard, stack logs or clean a shed.

Things went quite well until the second ditch
Where wheels began to spin --- we were On Stop.
Go back? Or leave it there? That was the choice.
I winded down the window, wiped the mirrors,
Engaged the diff-lock. Put it in reverse.
All went OK until the badger sett
When suddenly we slid right to the edge.
I had a look. It was not promising.
My right wheel was poised above the cliff.
The two back wheels were more or less all right.
The left hand front was on a pile of leaves.
I clambered out and worked my way along
By grabbing roots and clinging to the rocks.
Eventually climbed back to the track.
I stood behind my Land Rover. Assessed
The situation. Reckoned I could go
Another inch or two. Then re-assess.
I had another cautious little drive
And found I'd reached the final tipping point.
The choice was mine, alone. To walk away
And come back later with a winch and chain
Or take a chance and get it over with.

$\rightarrow$

My Land Rover is worth a quid or two
So if it fell it would be quite a loss.
Despite the fact that I am eighty three
There's still a few things I have left to do.
The wisest plan, I know, and knew it then,
Was play it safe, walk home and leave the sheep
Without their feed blocks for a day or two.
So I resolve, if such re-occurs,
I'll take the prudent path. Heed HSE.
Come back with help, a tractor, winch and chain.

But here I am. My Land Rover is too.
I promise to be sensible.
Next time.

Smiling Through

The wind has dropped, the sun is out ---
Don't need a coat if I go out ---
And if, worse luck, it starts to rain
I can go indoors again.

I've aches and pains, but when I tire
I often sit beside the fire
To read a book or watch TV ---
So many folk would envy me.

Once I was young, and now I'm old,
But never did what I was told.
My life's my own. I plan my day.
Some days I work, some days I play.

Lots of people find it funny
I manage on such little money ---
But I confess I have enjoyed
A lifetime being self employed.

Cataracts

Take me to a quiet estuary
Far from great rocks and raging cataracts,
I've had enough white water, racing streams
Where all is action without pause for rest.
I want to lie beside a sheltered bank
Where I can feel the tidal ebb and flow,
Let sun and moon define the time of day,
And if one morning I have sailed away
Don't look for me or waste a mournful tear.
I've had my turn, I cannot ask for more ---
Just feed the cats that come to my back door.

Glossary:

AMS   Automatic Milking System

Blagden   Romany term still used in the traveller community to describe a horse with white markings on the front and inner sides of the hind legs. Characteristic of heavy draught horses

Bushel   a volume measure of eight gallons. Four bushels of wheat weigh approximately two and a quarter hundredweight or nearly 120kg

Captain R E "Ronnie" Wallace MFH, born 1919 died in a road accident 2002

Cattle foil   areas where the scent of the fox is obscured by the scents of grazing cattle

Competitive Farming   by M G Cooper, Professor of Agriculture at Wye College, University of London, caused a considerable stir in the farming world in the early 1950's and became something of a cult book in the wider community

Couples   hounds are counted in couples

DCPF   Dynamic Concentrate Parlour Feeding.

EID   Electronic Identification. Required by law for all sheep and goats over twelve months of age

Feathering   1: plucking the feathers off a dead bird
                    2: hounds waving or twitching their sterns when they think they can smell a fox

GM   Genetically Modified

GPS   Global Positioning System

Hame   one of a pair of wooden or metal inserts to a horse harness collar to which the traces that pull the cart or implement are attached

HSE   Health and Safety Executive

Mask   hounds have heads, foxes have masks

Morfa   Welsh term for low-lying land behind the seashore

NPK   Nitrogen Phosphorous and Potassium, the main plant nutrients in chemical fertilizers

Paunched   gutted (viscera removed)

Quick   common alternative word for thorns

Ratcatcher   the least formal acceptable dress

Sallys   common alternative word for willows

Sewin   a term commonly used in Wales and Ireland for migratory sea trout

Shippon   old word for a shed in which cows are milked

Stern   dogs have tails, hounds have sterns

The field   mounted followers of the hunt. There is only one huntsman (or woman) who controls the hounds. The field, or followers, are in effect spectators

The poultry fund   a sum of money set aside to compensate farmers/smallholders for poultry (or lambs) killed by foxes to discourage shooting them

Walk   the parts of an unfenced mountain common on which different flocks graze. If undisturbed most sheep stick to their own walk most of the time

-oOOoo-